Hospital

May 1978

Rene, Sue, Dave & Sheri

Dunking Doughnuts

Dunking Doughnuts

A Fun Look at Life
Through the Verse of Leonhard Dowty
Illustrated by Peter Lippman

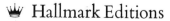 Hallmark Editions

EGO

If I were you,
I'd love me, too.

SOME PEOPLE

Some people!
You wonder if they're part of the human race
The way they let doors slam in your face.
Really!
Some of them are positively eely.

Such people
Don't deserve the courtesy of others,
No one could love them but their mothers.
Poor things,
Stuck with such inconsiderate offsprings.

Those people
Who practically knock you down in the elevator
Must think their hurry is much greater,
Or perhaps
They're not people at all but booby traps.

However,
The pushers and shovers, yankers and smackers
Usually wind up the way-in-the-backers.
So there!
Impolite people get absolutely nowhere.

THOUGHT PIECE

I wish I were a great thinker
Like Plato and Socrates and Aristotle,
Who never had a thought that was a clinker
Or had to use their brains full throttle.
(Me, I've got to think with all my might
Just to tell my left from right.)

Of course, they could wander quietly
    around the Acropolis
Or meditate in Grecian glades
Where I contend with the noisy metropolis,
Construction and parades.
(I am not against parades as such,
Except that they occur too much.)

They, those wise and thoughtful Greeks,
Could patiently wait upon the Muse,
Who came to them with rosy cheeks
And gave them all her views, including the latest news.
(Me, I sit and wait and wait
And, if she comes at all, she's late.)

Those ancient thinkers didn't worry about money.
Their clothes were but drafty sheets.
People gave them little cakes dripping with honey
And, to the Olympic games, aisle seats.
(Me, I'd look silly wrapped in a sheet.
I've too much trouble making ends meet.)

Oh, those boys, they really had it easy.
All day they just sat around and thunk.
People brought them gifts from Zambesi
And Rhodes and Phoenician ships they had sunk.
(Me, I work for all I get.
I cast my bread and it comes back wet.)

I'd be able to think, too,
If I didn't have anything else to do.
Wouldn't you?

ODE TO A MARTINI

How sharper than a serpent's tooth
Is a jigger of gin and a dash of vermouth.

A DICTIONARY OF LOVE

Love is a mad, tempestuous thing,
Love is a tender caress,
Love is a daffodil in spring,
Love is a total mess.
Love is as calm as the Pacific,
As wild as the Atlantic,
Sometimes terrific,
Sometimes plain frantic.
Love is holding hands and sharing sodas,
Breathing sighs and rubbing noses.
Love is fortissimos, crescendos and codas,
Love is a bower of roses.
Love is this, Love is that,
Not knowing where you're at.
Whether you leave it or take it,
Love is what you make it.

YES, MY DARLING DAUGHTER

Our house is filled with many joys:
A playful pup, a pair of boys,
A fireside warm and cozy,
An easy chair soft and dozy,
Quilts and spreads from Grandma's attic,
Lots of gadgets automatic
That wash and whisk and whip and whirl—
And one enchanting little girl.
A quiet child with enormous eyes
As round as the world and blue as the skies,
A golden girl of exceptional beauty
With a rare and special sense of duty.
When she crawls into my lap and gives me a hug,
I'm useless as a doodlebug,
And when she kisses me upon the cheek,
The world is my oyster, so to speak.
Her mother thinks that I'm often inclined
To lose perspective, to be a bit blind,
But I really don't think it's entirely true—
I mean, honest and truly, her eyes *are* that blue!
And her laughter . . . it's like singing birds,
Temple bells . . . well, there are no words!
Surrounded by dolls (there are fifty or more),
She's a miniature mommy in a plaid pinafore,
Serving up tea and make-believe sweets
To make-believe ladies in make-believe seats,
Cleaning the table and washing the dishes
As though cups and saucers were magical wishes.

Would that I could catch her a star,
Or put the moon in a jelly jar.
Would that I could capture a dream,
Give her a mountain, a rainbow, a stream.
Like hundreds of fathers since time was hatched,
I find myself completely unlatched,
An easy ploy, as weak as water,
A willing pawn for my perfect daughter.

RHYMES WITH REASON

Car Pool
A system of modern transportation,
Person to person and station to station.

To a Sick Friend
Mended?
Splendid!

OBSERVATION

There is nothing moister
Than an oyster.

A LIZARD'S LAMENT

I'm lizard, chameleon true,
Lizard born, lizard grew,
And my parents were pure lizard, too.

I'm lizard from pink tongue to tail,
Complete lizard, Sauria male,
Weighing, stripped, one ounce plus on the scale.

But it's not so important what a lizard weighs
As how a good lizard spends his days.

Mostly he lies aleaf in the sun
Snatching flies one by one,
Which is highly indigestible and not much fun.

Just to vary things a bit,
He changes color for the heck of it—
For a lizard, prerequisite.

But I don't want to bore you with trivial data.
The point of my story's considerably greater.

I'm a lizard, a fact I abhor.
Being a lizard's an absolute bore.
(Just try it sometime and see what's in store.)

You're mortal, pure Homo sapien,
A state I'd be quite happy in,
Anything but lizard, which you can only be nappy in.

In your world, where I wish I'd been put,
Grass seems to be greener on some other foot.

Well, it isn't, I'm here to tell.
Loafing all day is positive hell.
You've progress to make and products to sell.

We lizards sometimes hear people say
"Boy, what a life, sleeping all day."
Well, I'll tell you, my friend, I'll trade you. Okay?

I'll take your taxes, your job and your beef.
You catch the flies and lie on my leaf.

RHYMES WITH REASON

Pets
Any of the quadrupeds
Found asleep in children's beds.

Kisses
Expressions of endearment,
(Sometimes flavored spearmint).

A Friend
That rare and special human being
With whom you find yourself
   agreeing.

CURRENT TRENDS
(Or Caught Short on the Electric Circuit)

Oh, wonderful age of electrical science!
We haven't a room without an appliance.
Though ours is but a simple cottage,
We've got tons and tons of wattage.
From radio clocks to suntan lamps,
Our lives are ruled by volts and amps.
An electrical roaster cooks the roast.
An electrical toaster browns the toast.
Machines both wash and iron our duds.
Our dishes get scrubbed in electrical suds.
TV brings us dramas eclectic.
We polish our shoes with brushes electric.
We alter a dial and, lo and behold,
A room that was hot is suddenly cold.
We've twice as much current as electric eels
In this marvelous age of electrical meals.
Our chicken is fried in electrical pans.
Electric contraptions open tin cans.
Our coffee is perked by electrical means.
Soup is kept warm in electric tureens.
Electrical juicers squeeze out the juice.
Electric devices help us reduce.
Electrical clippers trim back the hedge.
Electrical sharpeners keep knives on edge.
Electrical magic brings to our home
Waxers and buffers to brighten the chrome,

Blankets electric to spend the night snug in,
All sort of things to snap on and plug in:
Heaters and freezers, vacuums and drills,
Razors and clippers and barbecue grills,
Hi-Fi equipment (woofers and tweeters),
Mixers and blenders, grinders and beaters,
Sewing machines that work by a switch,
Electrical doodads for scratching an itch.
Now all that we need to round out our gear
Is a sleep-in electrical home engineer.

THOUGHTS OF HOME

Home is where the heart is,
Where the children's
    scribbled art is,
Where the random blocks
    and skates are,
Where the socks without
    their mates are.
Home is where the bills are,
Where the fevers
    and the chills are,
Where the crumbs of bread
    and cakes are,
Where no one knows the rakes are.
Home is where the weeds grow,
Where all except the seeds grow,
Where the dogs and frogs
    and cats are,
Where the scratches, cuts
    and spats are.
Home is where the salami is
And, thank heaven, where
    the mommy is.

CHRISTMAS MAIL

Dear Santa Claus,
I am writing you because
I have seen what I want at Saks—
A pair of blue velvet slacks,
Pale blue, the color of heaven,
No pockets, size eleven;
An alligator bag and matching shoes,
A pair of diamond cockatoos,
A feather boa in white or pink,
A beaver hat trimmed with mink,
A nice big bottle of Miss Dior,
An ermine coat that sweeps the floor,
And any other little bauble that captures your fancy.
Until then—Love, Nancy.

MMMMmmmmm

I love the letter M.
M, as in Magic and Mystery and Mirth.
Although I'm fond of A and D and Z and the rest,
The letter M is truly the best,
The salt of the earth,
A gem
With its two Marvelous, Mountaintop peaks,
Mu, twelfth letter of the Magnificent Greeks.
Think of it,
Clear your throat and drink of it.
Taste it like champagne:
M as in Mercury and Mars and Millinocket, Maine,
The M of the Mythical Muses,
The Myriad of M's that history uses:
Muhammad, Minsky, Mountbatten,
Mississippi, Moses, Manhattan,
Dozens and dozens and dozens of them,
Uncles and aunts and cousins of them.
Take Music, for example—
Mendelssohn and Mozart and Mary Martin.
M's a letter you can put your heart in,
A letter to savor,
To favor,
To sample
Like some exquisite Mousse
Or a Melon oozing delectable juice.
Think of Moonlight
On a bright Mediterranean night,

Of Morning, early
Magnolias, pearly.
Let your Mind (ah, there's an M
To reckon with the best of them!)
Wander into March, the start of spring,
And Masterpieces by Michelangelo and Matisse.
(The wonders of M never cease.)
If not of March, imagine May
And the kind of Merry, Madcap day
That makes Minstrels sing.
Oh, and bring me Miranda, Miranda, Miranda,
So the two of us can sit upon the veranda,
Miranda and Me,
Me and Miranda,
Me kneeling at her Maidenly hem,
Worshipping the letter M.

WATCH THE BIRDIE

The duck is a creature that flies and swims,
According to that moment's whims—
That is, whenever he wishes
He swims with the fishes,
Except he swims on top of the water
Instead of beneath it, where he oughta.
Then if he decides to fly,
He spreads his wings and it's birdie, bye bye.
No baggage to pack, no clothing to squeeze in.
He goes as he is to the Florida Keys in.
With just a few feathers and a bit of luck,
You, my friend, could have been a duck.

LOVE SONG

I love you more than the Nile has miles,
More than the Mona Lisa smiles,
More than the Alps have snow-covered peaks,
More than a baby has pink in its cheeks.

I love you more than the rain is wet,
More than the sum of the national debt,
More than diapers are folded and pinned,
And not a bit less than the devil has sinned.

I love you more than Alaska is cold,
More than King Midas treasured his gold,
More than a flush has beaten a straight,
Considerably more than an elephant's weight.

I love you more than turtles need shells,
More than a llama needs double l's,
More than the British sing "God Save the Queen,
More than Cole Porter began the beguine.

I love you more than a radar has blips,
I love you more than Flipper flips,
More than Roebuck is coupled with Sears,
More than they duel in "The Three Musketeers."
I love you more than the stretch of elastic.
I love you so much—it's really fantastic!

LOVER'S LAMENT

That summer was the summer of Anne,
As blond as wheat,
Brown-eyed, sweet,
Laughter-filled, eighteen and tan,
A girl to turn the heart of any man.
And turn my heart she did, she did.
It flipped and flopped.
It nearly stopped.
But when I made my smitten bid,
Within my chest I heard it skid.
"Too young, too young," was her reply.
I shook my head.
My heart played dead.
Ice and sleet invaded July.
Too young for love, too old to cry.
So there I stood—disqualified—
When I was ten and the world too wide.

COMPANY MANNERS

In certain books of etiquette
The social rules are firmly set
Regarding things that one should do
As well as those proclaimed taboo.

For example, slacks don't go
At banquets where they serve shad roe
And unshod feet create a breach
Anywhere but at the beach.

Soup, of course, should not be heard.
Dunking doughnuts is absurd.
Snakes and such should not be charmed,
Nor should aces e'er be palmed.

Childhood friends should not be shot,
Cantaloupe not served hot,
Nor should gum be thrown in streets,
Stuck on ears or under seats.

Pinky out when sipping tea;
Hair in place when up a tree;
Coat and tie when at the Ritz;
Smile on face when winner quits.

Bigger smile for hole in one;
Lavish praise for jobs well done;
Pluck and grit when in the thick;
Apologies for trumping trick.

Good firm clasp when shaking hands;
Modesty at Baby Grands;
Sympathy for friends who ail;
Saw and files for friends in jail.

All these things let it be said
Inform your friends that you're well bred.
And tell them too that you're not green
To Emily Post's social sheen.

You've got luster; you've got class,
Seldom rude, never crass.
You reflect the uppermost,
Whether guest, whether host.

SPRING SONG

Spring is the season that's golden,
The season nobody gets cold in,
Of gay flowered hats
And sunny cravats
And weather you cannot feel old in.

Spring is the season we thrive in,
The season we all feel alive in,
The time of the year
To be a pioneer
With all of the country to drive in.

Spring is the season that's joyous,
The season for men to feel boyous,
The season for girls
To fluff up their curls,
When nothing on earth can annoy us.

Spring is the season for wishing,
The time when we want to go fishing,
The season we dream
Of finding a stream
Just made for our feet to go swishing.

Spring is the season to play in,
The season we wish we could stay in,
The season that brings
The flutter of wings
And hundreds of things to be gay in.

Spring is the season of plenty,
The season when everything's scenty,
The season when folks
Get rid of their yokes
And tend to feel fresh, young and twenty!

SYMPHONY FOR A BOY

Bang on the cymbals,
Play on the lutes,
He finally learned
To hang up his suits.

Blow on the trumpets,
Toot on the flutes,
He stops at the door
And scrapes off his boots.

Pluck on the harp,
Beat on the drum,
It's taken so long
I'm struck deaf and dumb.

HOW DO I LOVE THEE?

How do I love thee? Let me count the ways.
I love thee in blue jeans and black negligees.
I love thee in old pj's with rabbit-fur slippers,
In housecoats and beach coats, snorkel and flippers.
I love thee with cold cream all over your face,
In calico aprons and clouds of white lace,
In department stores, stadiums and discount houses,
In plain cotton shirts and dotted Swiss blouses,
With earrings that dangle and hairdos that tower,
Up to your shoulders in soapsuds or flour.
I love thee in prints with daisies and lilies,
In Kalamazoo or the Greater Antilles,
In gowns of silk and shimmering satin,
Letting the dog out and letting the cat in,
Taking the children to school or to church,
Broiling a flounder or frying a perch,
Dressed to the nines for a dinner at eight,
Looking superb, serene and sedate,
Calling to Joey, Michael and Teddy,
"All right, you kids, dinner is ready!"
And serving it up as though you wore taffeta.
I love you, my love, because I just haffeta.

MY SON, MY SON

We've a boy in our house, a peach of a fellow
Who'd live, if permitted, on raspberry Jell-O,
Who'd never wear shoes unless it was snowing,
Who flies through the house with the speed of a Boeing.
His pockets can hold, all at one time,
A sandwich, a frog, six snails and a dime,
Which doesn't include the things he may garner
On brief expeditions from home to the corner.
Like all other boys, ours can be noisy.
Friends have reported they've heard him in Boise.
Though this is not true, it's close to the truth—
He's only been heard as far as Duluth.
His knees are a mass of bruises and scratches.
The seat of his jeans has patches on patches.
He cannot sit still for more than a minute.
When mud is around, he's got to get in it.
Not that he's bad, he's simply all boy—
A door-slamming, windjamming bundle of joy
Who looks like his mother with great saucer eyes
Where innocence lies in eternal surprise.
He's bright as a button, a genius, of course;
But that was expected, with *us* as the source.
The questions he asks are deep and complex:
Things about space and science and sex,
Things about pilots, boxers and dancers,
Questions to which we haven't the answers.
Dressed up for church, he looks like a saint,
Though five minutes later it's clear that he ain't,

For in that short span he's climbed up a pole
Or hidden himself in his favorite hole.
Perhaps I've depicted too much of a terror.
If this is the case, I admit to my error,
For what we have got is a frisky bull calf,
Not just a boy but a boy and a half.

ALL THE KING'S HORSES

A long time ago in your childhood,
    you heard of a fatal fall,
The tumble of poor Humpty Dumpty
    from high on a battery wall.
Poor Humpty was obviously dreaming,
    not thinking of whereon he sat,
Until he heard himself screaming
    and came down to earth with a splat.
They called out the mighty king's army,
    the navy, the Wacs and marines,
But nought could they do to pull Humpty through
    with all of their medical means.
A moral there is to the story,
    a moral worth heeding by all:
Though dreaming is nice, it doesn't suffice
    for keeping your eye on the ball.

FLORAL ARRANGEMENT

Beloved, thou hast brought me flowers,
Bright posies that have cheered my darkest hours:
Violets of a royal shade
That only heaven could have made,
And chrysanthemums
As bold as national anthenums,
And smiling pansies and forget-me-nots
And lilies with tiger spots
And sweet peas and peonies and phlox
In a brightly ribboned florist box.
And roses, red as ruby wine—
Divine, divine!
Magnolia, enough to cover me all over,
And sweetly scented Yankee clover.
But, oh, my dearest harlequin,
Please find a vase to put them in.

FANFARE FOR FATHER

Fathers are exceptional creatures
Who inhabit armchairs and hammocks and bleachers.
Never placid or acid or humdrum,
It's the male of the species they come from.
That is to say they're of masculine gender—
The sex which denies that its nature is tender.
Fathers are a credit to all *Homo sapiens*—
Indians, Spaniards, Germans and Lappians.
They hail from such places as Portland and Macon
And work very hard to bring home the bacon.
You can tell that they're different from mammas
By the size of their hats and pajamas.
They're tougher and stricter and stronger
And the reach of their arms is much longer.
These grown-up Tom Swifts and Tom Sawyers
Make excellent doctors and lawyers,
Tailors and sailors, whalers and draftsmen,
Salesmen, accountants and all kinds of craftsmen.
All fathers have whiskers and some have mustaches.
Theirs are the pockets where all the loose cash is.
Theirs are the heads where most of the brains are.
Theirs are the backs where most of the pains are.
No one is better at fractions and numbers.
No one is sadder at waltzes and rhumbas.
They're handy with hammers, chisels and pliers,
Bevels and levels and barbecue fires.
A father's the whole family's hero—
Part Lindbergh, part Tarzan, part Nero.

He has, it is clear, the patience of Job
And he's happiest wearing his slippers and robe.
As head of the house, he foots the bills
For chops and tops and coated pills,
For lamps and stamps and towels and sheets
And hats and bats and parakeets.
Give him a gift—say, a pipe or a belt—
And right on the spot a father will melt.
He'll listen in silence to most people's views,
But he'll argue like mad at the six o'clock news.
Fathers are sometimes extremely outspoken,
Especially on days when they're rudely awoken,
But soon as they see that chip off the block
They're inclined to forget the hands of the clock.
Though they can't ever find their socks or their specs,
Fathers are really a marvelous sex,
Happy-go-lucky, thoughtful of others,
The very best things to be married to mothers.

RHYMES WITH REASON

Marriage
That honorable institution
   in which
Some people would rather fight
   than switch.

Courtship
An ancient custom, probably
   Greek,
Based upon the game of Hide
   and Seek.

Envy
A not very pleasant human habit,
When she has a mink and you
   have rabbit.

A WISE FATHER

Our youngest son's a question mark
From whom his elders flee,
For he would know of light and dark
And wind and sand and sea.
Why, he asks with eyes that yearn,
Do clocks have hands instead of feet?
And he, from me, would like to learn
What makes molasses sweet?
Why does a rainbow form an arch?
How far does space extend?
Why does April follow March?
Where does a circle end?
Who invented the wheel and the cart?
Why do lizards creep?
Where is the break in a broken heart?
What makes willows weep?
I brace myself and answer these
In one way or another,
The best of which is simply, "Please,
Take that one to your mother."

FIRST LOVE

I have no mind for history's dates.
I cannot name the fickle Fates.
But I remember Jenny.

I can't recall at all, at all
Why Caesar ever wanted Gaul,
But I remember Jenny.

For Jenny, you see,
Thought highly of me,
When gumballs were two for a penny.

CHRISTMAS MAIL

Dear Gattling, Wister and Sloan:
Have you ever tried reaching your store
   by phone?
I'm glad, of course, that you're doing
   such a nice Christmas trade,
But I'm afraid
A mistake has been made.
We didn't order your genuine English
   marmalade,
And although we dearly love it—
Eight cases of it!???
You see, there is just my husband and I,
And what we ordered was one (1)
   gentleman's tie,
A very conservative, sincere type—
Black, with a tiny gray stripe.
We saw it in your window just last week
Adorning the bust of some curly-haired
   Greek—
Homer, maybe, or Socrates.
And the tie is what we'd like, please.
Hopefully—but not very—
I am trying to remain, Mrs. Judson
   T. Terry.

SHELL GAME

"Step right up and try your luck,"
The pitchman told the local cluck.
"Just place your bet and—one, two, three—
Pick the shell that hides the pea."
The yokel watched with careful eye.
He'd heard that pitchmen's ways were sly,
But not a thing could he detect
That seemed amiss or incorrect.
Each time the pitchman hid the pea,
The yokel knew where it would be.
Each time he guessed, he guessed just right.
(Pretty soon the fish would bite.)
And bite he did! He swallowed whole
The hook, the line, the fishing pole.
He placed his money on the line.
The pitchman's eyes began to shine.
Buck by buck, the callous cad
Took each bill the yokel had—
Ones and twos and fives and tens,
Not to mention pigs and hens,
Butter, milk, eggs and spuds,
All he took, including duds.
Oh, what fools we mortals be
To seek the shell that hides the pea
And, knowing better, enter in
A game Houdini couldn't win.

TO CINDY, WHO'S THREE

In February's gloom,
You bloom.
Although the day
Is cold gray
And unsmiling,
You bring
The warmth of May
Into a room,
Enchanting and beguiling.
What a precious thing
You are:
A breath of spring,
An evening star,
And mine,
Divine,
My forever valentine.

CHRISTMAS MAIL

Dear Mr. Palooza of Lalla Palooza Toys:
Someone sent one of our boys
A deluxe model of your plastic pachyderm—
(What would be an elephant in some other firm).
Since March, we have been trying to assemble it
And what we've got doesn't faintly resemble it.
The box says there are 2,572 separate parts . . .
But does an elephant really have seven hearts?
We are also short one tusk (Part II, Section B),
Designed to fit snugly into slot 943,
Only slot 943 is somewhere in the rear quarters,
Where the clasp would be if an elephant wore garters.
Naturally, our boy is disappointed,
Having an elephant so disjointed.
So please, could you arrange
To make an exchange?
We'll take something simple, all in one piece,
Nothing to glue, nothing to crease,
No parts to fit in unwelcoming slots,
No staples, no screws, no "easily tied" knots.
For this we shall bless you in all of our prayers
And I'll try to remain . . .T. Singleton Ayres.

THE HOUSEWIFE

Women, they say, are the weaker sex,
Simple-minded, nervous wrecks,
No match for men in brain or brawn.
But who gets up at crack of dawn
To start the coffee perking
Long before her sleeping spouse
   has cocked an eye at working?
While he has dreams to caper in,
Who brings the morning paper in?
Half-asleep on still-tired legs,
Who squeezes juice and scrambles eggs,
And, agile as an ath-e-lete,
Runs from toast to Cream of Wheat,
Turning bacon as she goes—
A perfect act for Ringling Bros.?

Even on her day of rest,
Who gets the children up and dressed?
Who shines their shoes and darns their socks?
Who nurses them through chicken pox?
Who's in charge of pocket tissues,
Stomach-aches and moral issues,
Mislaid mittens, wayward caps,
Malted milks and gingersnaps?
Who's part-time doctor, full-time tailor,
Letter-writer, package mailer,
Ironer, washer, drier of tears,
Waxer of tables and chiffoniers?

Who calls the plumber, the cleaner, the vet?
Who changes diapers whenever they're wet?

Who plans the meals to everyone's tastes,
Lets down the hems and lets out the waists?
Who winds the clocks and sets the alarm?
Who closes the windows in case of a storm?
Who gives the parties? Who makes the dates?
Who stands and serves and who also waits?
Who cleans the closets, the books and the shelves,
Pretends to be monkeys, soldiers and elves,
Fired at by hunters, riddled by guns,
Stepped on and slept on and captured by Huns?
Who, when it rains, is the teller of tales
Of wizards and witches and windjamming whales?
Who is the queen of the broom and the mop?
Who knows what is needed and just where to shop?

Who shines the silver, the copper and brass?
Who fills the tank when the car's out of gas?
Who makes the curtains, fluffs up the pillows,
Tends to the roses and waters the willows?
Who puts out the cat and lets in the dog?
Who feeds the turtle, the fish and frog?
Who wraps the presents? Who saves the cord?
Who never spends more than *they* can afford?
Who vacuums rugs, who makes the beds,
Who cuts the toenails and washes the heads?
Who drags in the bikes, the sleds and the wagons?
Who chases nightmares infested with dragons?

Who, without fail, attends PTA?
Who picks up pajamas and puts them away?

Who is the keeper of snorkels and flippers,
Knitter of sweaters, replacer of zippers,
Patcher of pockets, buyer of stamps,
Scrubber of tiles and duster of lamps?
Who puts whose slippers in front of whose chair?
Who's sweet as a lamb when he's gruff as a bear?
Who tints and bleaches, sprinkles and starches?
Whose spirits don't fall but, oh, her poor arches?
Who is the lawyer who settles all quarrels?
Who is dispenser of spankings and laurels?
Who, for the dolls, sews miniature dresses?
Surely by now you don't need three guesses.
Woman, of course—that stanch household betterer
Whose life is a round of incessant *et cetera*.

RHYMES WITH REASON

Space Program
Closets are something there is always a lack of,
And in which everything you want is always in back of.

Observation
Love is something a woman dotes on
And a psychiatrist gets rich taking notes on.

TO A PAMPERED WIFE

Indeed this very love which is my boast
Is the self-same love that burned the toast
And made a mockery of last night's mutton.
She cannot, for love's own sweet sake,
Make a bed or bake a cake
Or iron a shirt or sew a simple button.
But, oh, I love this good for nutton.

A LOVE REMEMBERED

Once when the world was new to me,
Made of paper, paint and glue to me,
A boy carved a crooked heart upon a crooked tree
And in its middle wrote, "Tommy T. loves Mary C."
We were young, as alive as spring.
The world was ours on a colored string.
We looked upon that crooked heart
As though it were a work of art,
A masterpiece given life
By a boy, a girl and a Boy Scout knife.
But the world grew up and so did we,
And so as well did the crooked tree.
Tommy and I went separate ways.
Summers we swam in different bays,
Winters we found respective joys
With other girls and other boys.
I remember after all these years
How he crossed his eyes and wiggled his ears.
I remember the dimple that flashed in his chin,
And the Sunday-school play when he was Huck Finn.
I remember his eyes, dark with a snap,
And hair that peeked out from a baseball cap.

We laugh about it now, each with our mate,
About how we swung as one on the garden gate
And laughed as one at funny things
And gave each other paper rings.
Nothing happened; we just grew apart;
But not the tree from the crooked heart.
It stands there still, that timeless bark
Where puppy love has left its mark.

CHRISTMAS MAIL

Dear Grandma Hayes,
Thank you for the lovely sachets.
There is nothing to cheer up blue Mondays
Like a bit of verbena in one's undies.
Next year, though, could you make it rose,
Since verbena makes my nose
Itch and my eyes water.
Appreciatively, Granddaughter.

MIRROR, MIRROR

Can you find yourself here in the crowd?
Are you one of the smiling or gloomily-browed?
Are you of the sort whose mouth droops and sags?
Are your eyes merely porters to carry the bags?
Do you look like a cherub? Do you look like a crow?
Are you something right out of the stories of Poe?
Do you look like a sinner or more like a saint?
Do you look like yourself or someone you ain't?
Do people around you feel gay when you're there
Or are you the kind who gets in their hair?
Do you scowl? Do you sneer? Do you constantly gripe?
Or are you the lovable, good-natured type?
Is interest revealed by the look on your face
Or while someone's talking are you off in space?
Do people run when you draw near?
Or do they beam from ear to ear?
Look in the mirror. What do you see?
Someone reflected as you wish to be?
Your face is your fortune, believe it or not.
You may like another, but this one you've got.
You can't change its features, you can't swap it off.
And only a fool would dare chop it off.
There in that mirror the whole story lies.
The solution's quite simple for folks who are wise:
Don't wear a puss that's vinegar sour.
Present to the world a smiling sunflower!

ODE TO OCTOBER

O is for October days—
Burnished gold on country ways,
Crisp and clean and crystal clear,
Featherweight the atmosphere.

Sunny skies are far less hot;
Hill and dale are apricot.
Robins pack to make their trip
Past the grip of winter's nip.

Pumpkins grow round and fat,
Cider mellows in the vat
While Mama Bears and Papa Bears
Busily prepare their lairs.

In the sky a harvest moon
Floats in space, a big balloon
Drifting gently in the breeze,
Sitting on the tops of trees.

On the grid the pigskin flies
Midst the cheers of old school ties.
All is zip and all is whiz.
That is what October is.

Everywhere within the O,
The days invite the heart to go
And take a magic carpet ride
Across the autumn countryside.

SPEAK TO ME OF LOVE

Don't talk to me of politics,
IBM or the New York Knicks.
Speak to me of love.
Tell me not of astrojets,
Foreign cars or office bets.
Speak to me of love.
Tell me how your heart goes thump,
Not about your Diesel pump.
Whisper words into my ear,
Sweet nothings I adore to hear,
And I will promise, cross my heart,
Not a word of works of art,
The children's school, the PTA,
A cunning frock or negligee
Or that I lost another glove,
If you will speak to me of love.

PACKAGED GOODS

I wonder what's in the gaily wrapped box.
Is it a coat with a collar of fox,
A fur that's fake but looks like mink,
A negligee of the laciest pink?
Perhaps it's a handbag of velvet or suede
Or another potholder the children have made.
Gloves—wrong size—of cotton or kid,
A pair of maracas handmade in Madrid?
Paris perfume of heavenly scent?
Inflatable houseboat, Arabian tent?
Whatever it is that lies inside,
I wish *it* wouldn't continue to hide,
For nothing is more annoyingly trapped
Than the "don't open" gift that is beautifully wrapped.

Set at the Castle Press in Bembo,
a Venetian face first cut in 1495 for the printer
Aldus Manutius Romanus and named by him in honor
of the humanist poet Pietro Bembo.
Printed on Hallmark Eggshell Book paper.